Celtic

Coloring Book

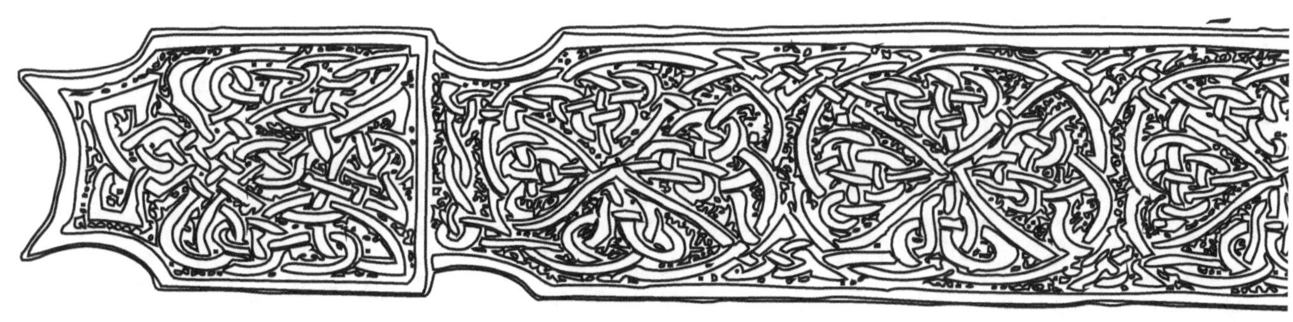

Celtic Coloring Book

This
Book
belongs to

Celtic Coloring Book

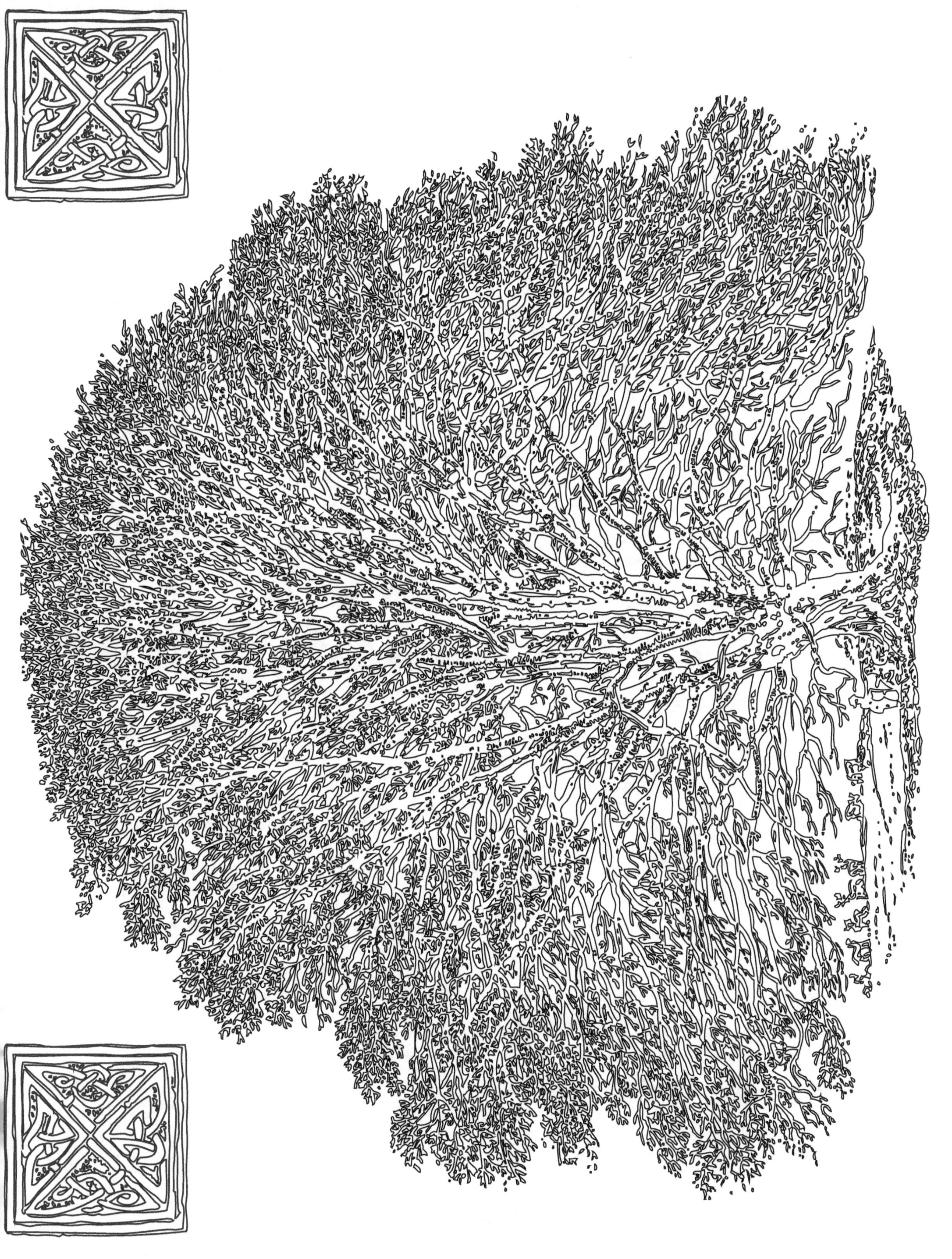

Celtic Coloring Book

Celtic Coloring Book

Celtic Coloring Book

Celtic Coloring Book

Celtic Coloring Book

Celtic Coloring Book

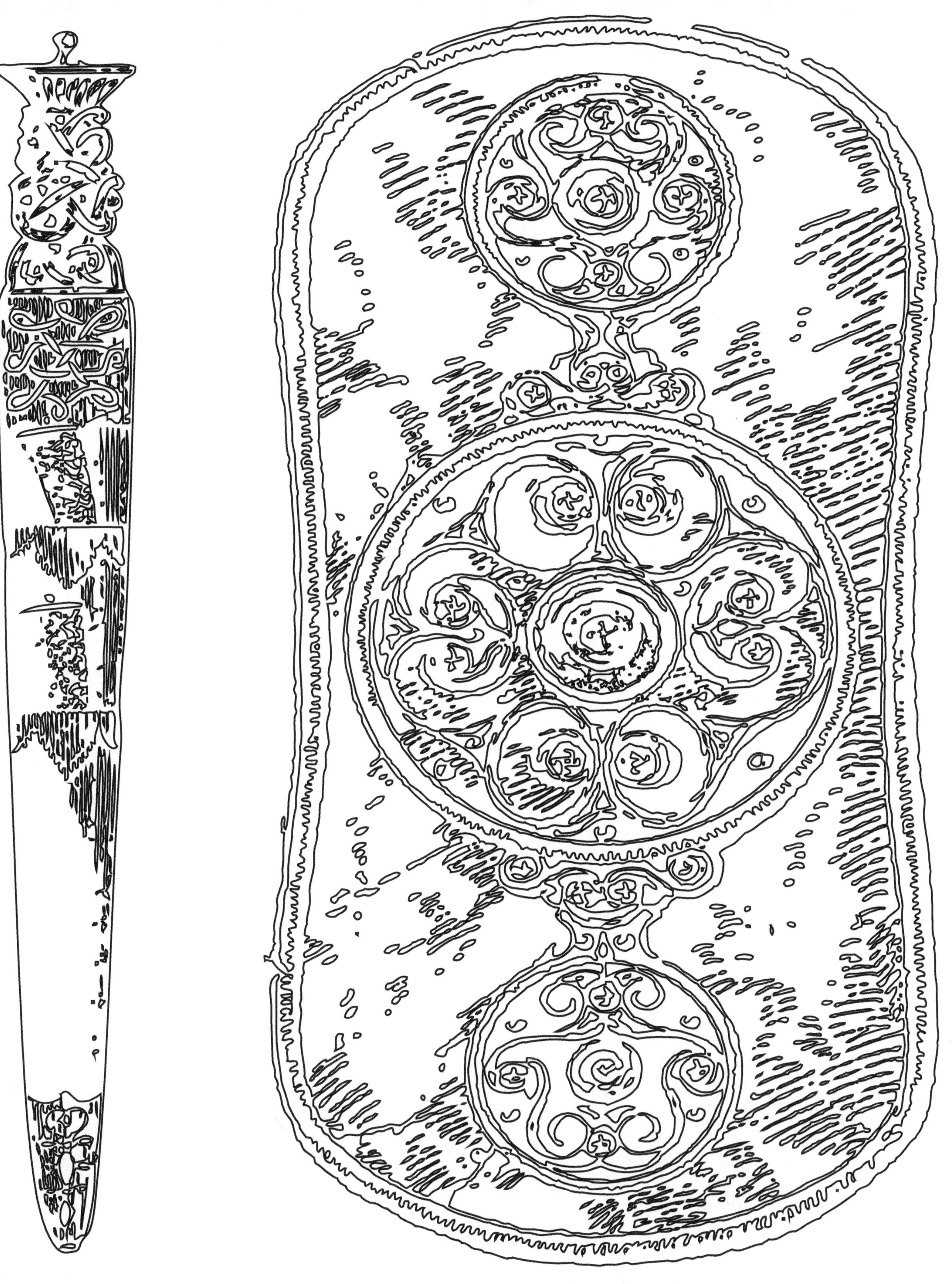

Celtic Coloring Book

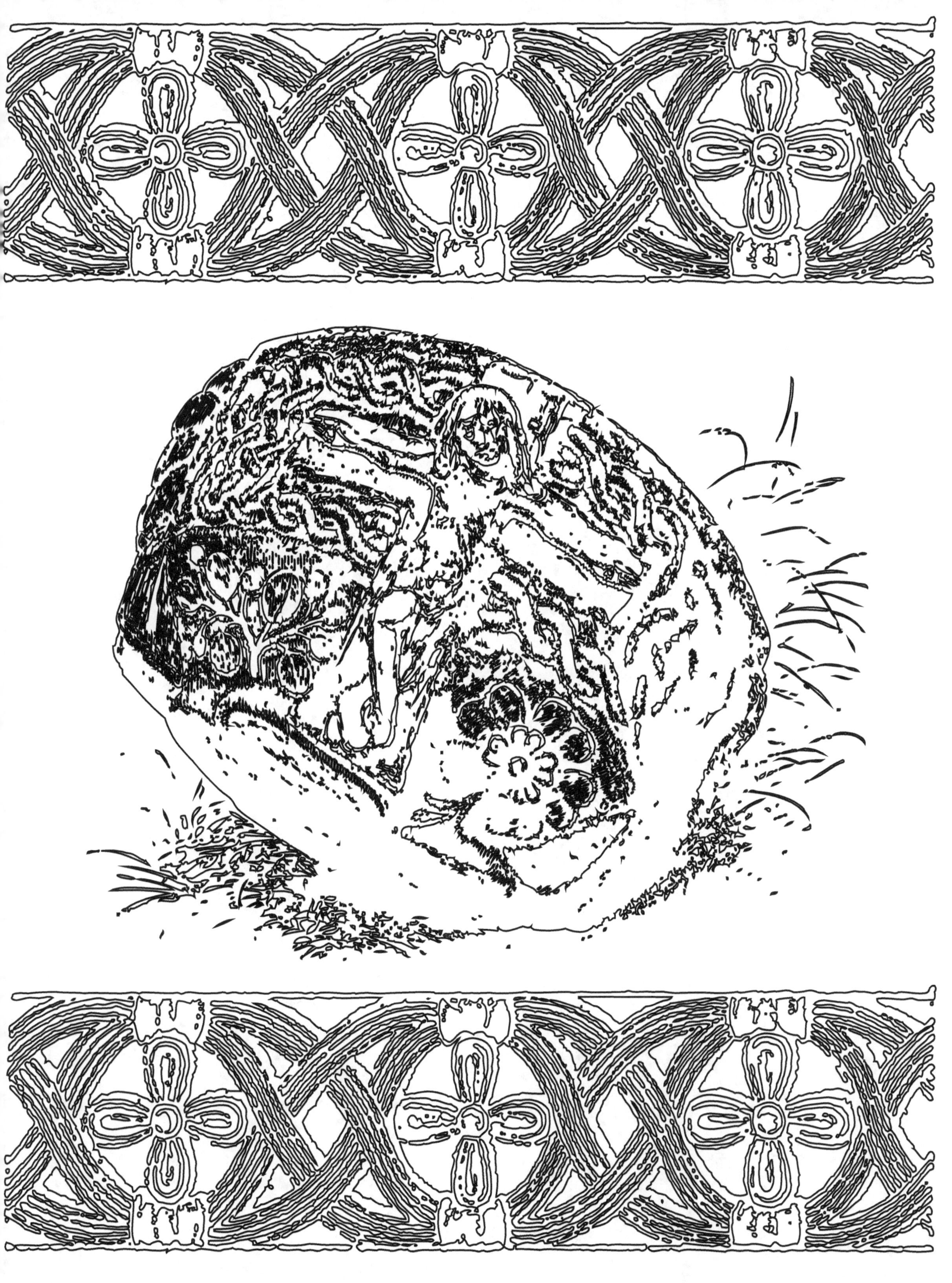

Celtic Coloring Book

Celtic Coloring Book

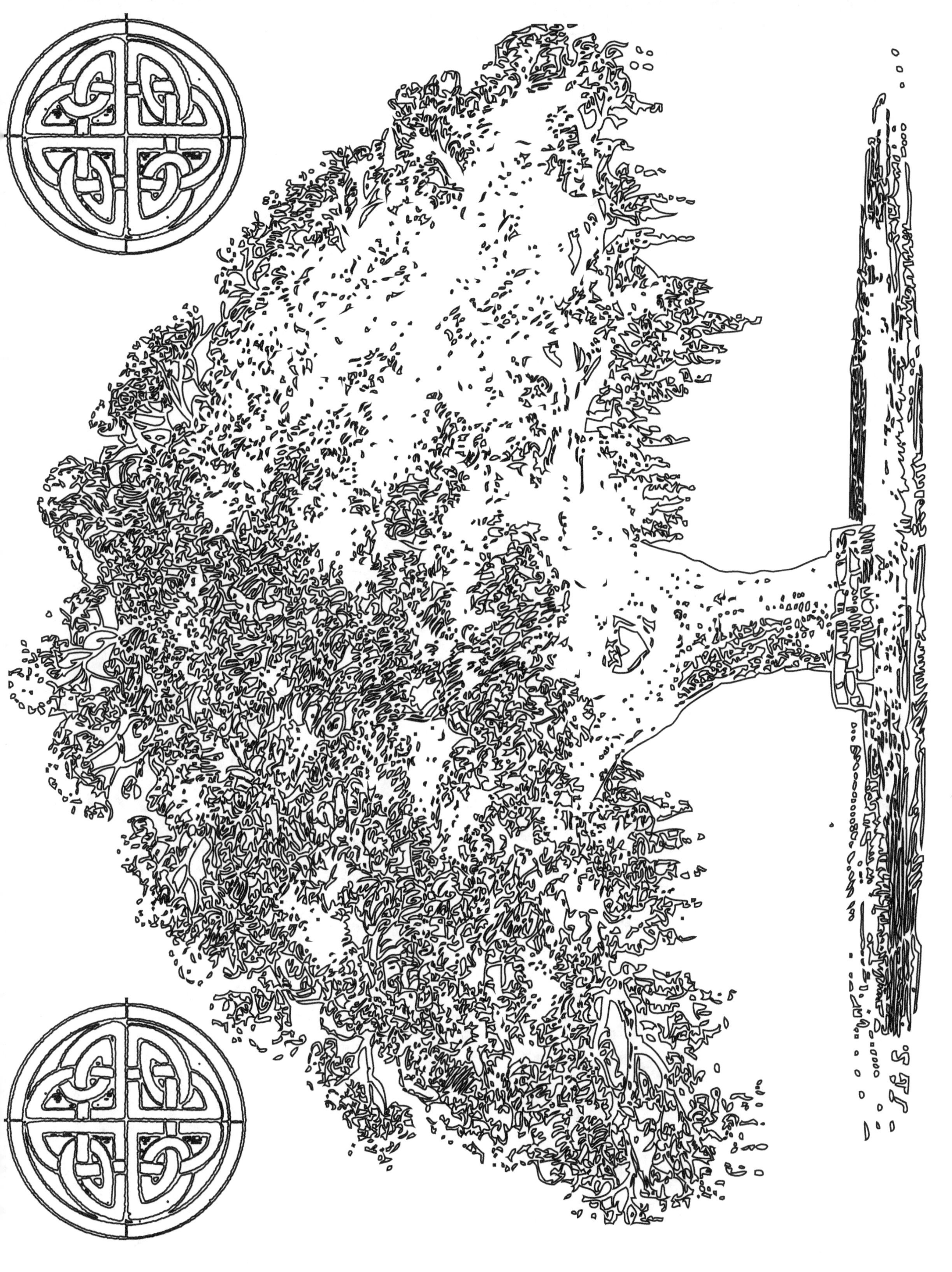

Celtic Coloring Book

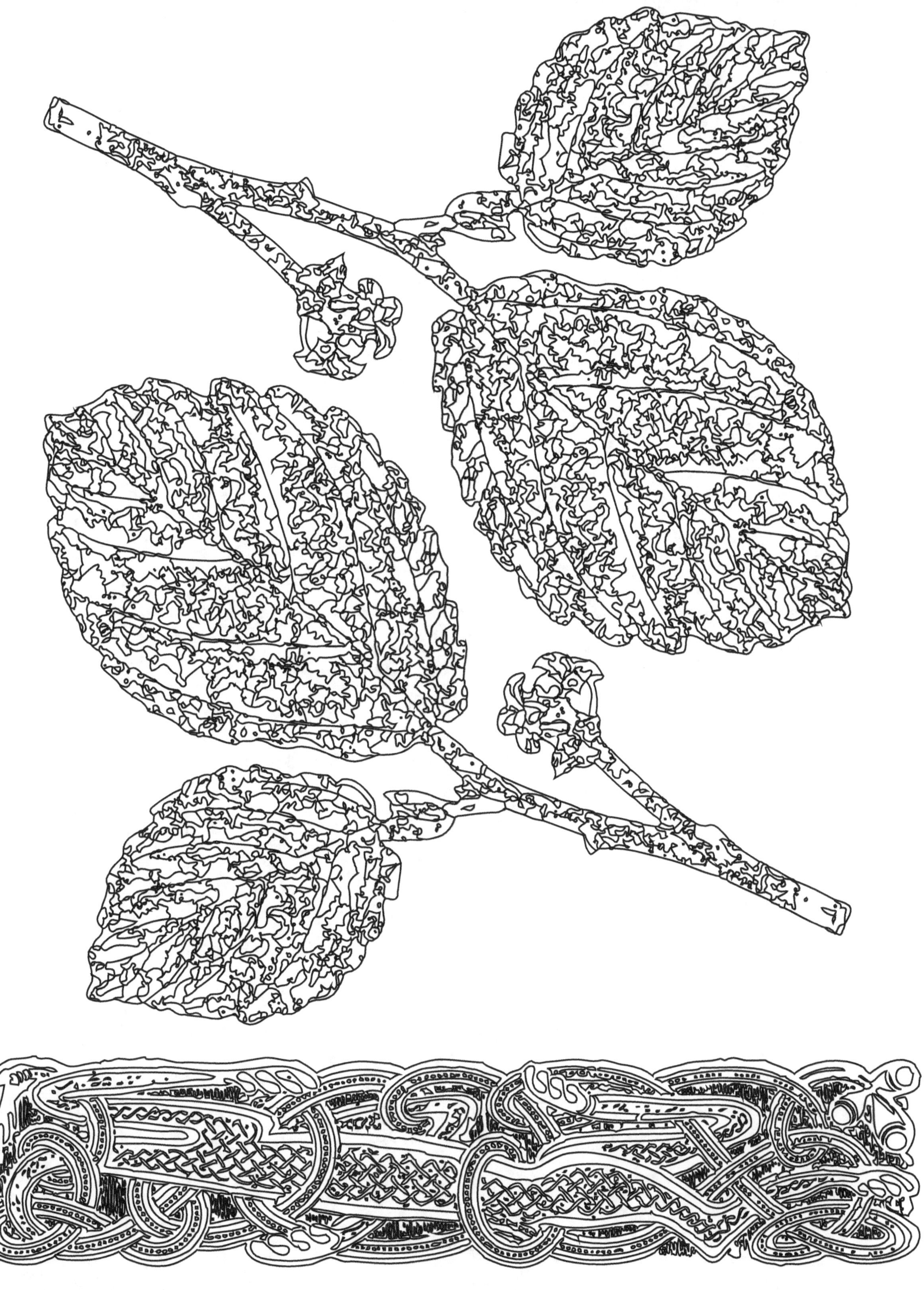

Celtic Coloring Book

Celtic Coloring Book

Celtic Coloring Book

Celtic Coloring Book

Celtic Coloring Book